Trumpet Ballads
By William Bay

WILLIAM BAY MUSIC

© 2015 by William Bay. All Rights Reserved.

Preface

The trumpet can be a beautifully lyrical instrument. Often not enough emphasis is placed on making the instrument sing. The 20 ballads contained in this book are designed to develop a lyrical sense. Play the pieces in a relaxed and free manner. Avoid playing too loud. On these pieces, when in doubt, play a notch softer than you might think normal. Strive for long phrases and let the melodies sing freely from your trumpet. I think that if you play a number of these ballads as part of your daily practice you will see a definite growth in your ability to play in a beautifully free style. I hope you enjoy playing them!

William Bay

Ballad #1

Ballad #2

William Bay

Ballad #3

William Bay

Ballad #4

Moderato ♩ = 112

William Bay

Ballad #5

William Bay

Ballad #6

William Bay

Ballad #7

William Bay

Ballad #8

Ballad #9

William Bay

Ballad #10

William Bay

Ballad #11

William Bay

Ballad #12

William Bay

Ballad #13

William Bay

Ballad #14

Moderately ♩ = 102

William Bay

Ballad #15

William Bay

Ballad #16

Ballad #17

William Bay

Ballad #18

William Bay

Ballad #19

Light and Flowing ♩ = 160

William Bay

Ballad #20

Andante ♩ = 80

William Bay

www.ingramcontent.com/pod-product-compliance
Lightning Source LLC
LaVergne TN
LVHW061320060426
835507LV00019B/2245